W9-CAL-053

IT'S ALL ABOUT...

SCARY SPIDERS

KINGFISHER
LONDON & NEW YORK

Copyright © Macmillan Publishers International Ltd 2015, 2021
First published in 2015 in the United States by Kingfisher
This edition published in 2021 by Kingfisher
120 Broadway, New York, NY 10271
Kingfisher is an imprint of Macmillan Children's Books, London
All rights reserved.

Distributed in the U.S. and Canada by Macmillan,
120 Broadway, New York, NY 10271

Library of Congress Cataloging-in-Publication data has been applied for

Series editor: Sarah Snashall
Series design: Little Red Ant and Laura Hall
Illustrations: Laura Hall
Adapted from an original text by Claire Llewellyn

ISBN 978-0-7534-7719-9

Kingfisher books are available for special promotions and premiums.
For details contact: Special Markets Department, Macmillan,
120 Broadway, New York, NY 10271

For more information, please visit www.kingfisherbooks.com

Printed in China
9 8 7 6 5 4 3 2 1
1TR/0521/WKT/UG/128MA

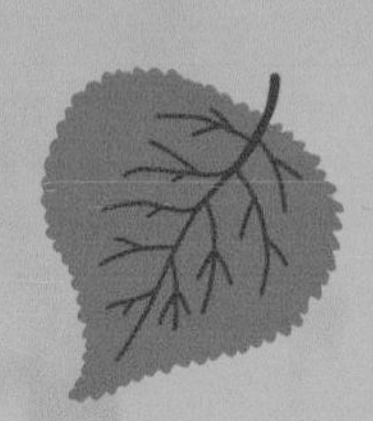

Picture credits
The Publisher would like to thank the following for permission to reproduce their material.
Top = t; Bottom = b; Center = c; Left = l; Right = r
Cover iStock/Thien Woei Jiing; Back cover Shutterstock/alslutsky; Pages 2–3, 6c, 30–31 Shutterstock/alslutsky; 4 Shutterstock/Tolchik; 5 Shutterstock/Audrey Snider-Bell; 7t Shutterstock/efendy; 7c Shutterstock/NoRegret; 7b Shutterstock/D Kucharski & K Kucharski; 8–9 Kingfisher Artbank; 9t Shutterstock/Audrey Snider-Bell; 9b Shutterstock/Will Howe; 10 Naturepl/Kim Taylor; 11 FLPA/Malcolm Schuyl; 12 Kingfisher Artbank; 13 Shutterstock/neelsky; 14 Shutterstock/Ian Grainger; 15t Shutterstock/Cathy Keifer; 15bl Shutterstock/Hulb Theunissen; 15br Shutterstock/Katarina Christenson; 16 Shutterstock/Fong Kam Yee; 17 Shutterstock/Jason Patrick Ross; 18 FLPA/Photo Researchers; 19t Naturepl/Stephen Dalton; 19b Shutterstock/Henrik Larsson; 20–21 Shutterstock/Nate A; 21t Shutterstock/Dr Morley Read; 21b Shutterstock/James van den Broek; 22–23 Shutterstock/Matteo photos; 23 Alamy/Zach Holmes; 24 Shutterstock/Kletr; 25 Shutterstock Kurt_G; 26–27 Shutterstock/Hue Chee Kong; 27t Naturepl/Premaphotos; 28t Alamy/Kristen Soper; 28 Shutterstock/Giuliano C. Del Moretto; 29 Corbis/Matthias Schrader/dpa.

Front cover: A jumping spider.

CONTENTS

For your free audio download go to

http://panmacmillan.com/audio/ScarySpiders

Happy listening!

Scan me!

Spiders everywhere	4
Spiders and friends	6
A spider's body	8
Spider silk	10
Wonderful webs	12
Killer fangs	14
Hunting prey	16
Ambush!	18
Deadly venom	20
Finding a mate	22
Spiderlings	24
Don't eat me!	26
Lovely spiders	28
Glossary	30
Index	32

Spiders everywhere

There are billions of spiders on Earth. They live in houses and gardens, ponds and caves, rain forests, deserts, and the Arctic. The only places where spiders can't live are Antarctica and the oceans.

Many spiders live in parks and gardens.

Spiders catch animals for food. The largest spiders eat snakes, lizards, and birds. The smallest ones eat tiny flies.

Record breaker:	world's largest spider
Leg span:	10 in. (25cm)
Effect of venom:	sickness, pain, and sweating
Eats:	insects, rodents, frogs

Raft spiders live near marshes and ponds.

Spiders and friends

Spiders have four pairs of legs and a body divided into two parts. Harvestmen, scorpions, mites, and ticks are in the same spider family. They are all called arachnids.

FACT ...

A spider is not an insect! Insects have three parts to their body and six legs. Most insects have antennae and wings; spiders never do.

Scorpions have a curved tail tipped with a sting.

Harvestmen look like spiders, but they do not spin silk.

Mites are tiny, with short legs and a round body.

A spider's body

A spider's body has two main parts: the head and the abdomen.

This spider leaves its old coat behind after it grows a new one.

Old coat

The whole body is covered with a tough, outer coat (called the exoskeleton). When the spider gets bigger, the coat bursts open.

Sharp fangs to inject venom

Palps are for tasting and feeling

SPOTLIGHT: Giant house spider

Famous for:	fastest spider
Leg span:	up to 4 in. (10cm)
Effect of venom:	harmless
Eats:	mites, mosquitoes, insects

Spider silk

Spider silk is stronger than steel and stretchy like elastic. It is waterproof and light enough to float.

Spiders use silk to build their webs, line their burrows, protect their eggs, and wrap up their prey.

A jumping spider leaps into the air from its safety line of silk.

A garden spider pulls the silk from its spinnerets to wrap up a fly.

A spider makes silk inside its body. The spider then uses one of its legs to pull and twist the different silk strands into a single, strong thread.

Wonderful webs

Many spiders make sticky webs to catch flies and other insects. Different types of spider spin different types of web.

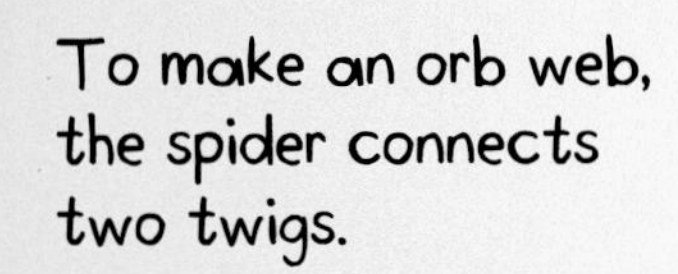

To make an orb web, the spider connects two twigs.

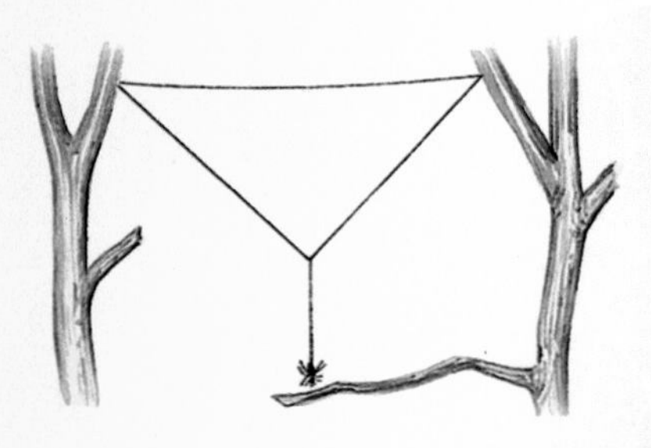

The spider adds spokes.

The spider spins a sticky spiral.

Most spiders spin a new web every day. The old one does not go to waste though; the spider eats it and recycles the silk.

Spotlight: Golden orb-weaver spider
Record breaker: largest orb web
Leg span: up to 2 in. (5cm)
Effect of venom: causes pain and redness
Eats: frogs and birds in its web

A helpless fly is rolled up in silk by a garden spider.

Killer fangs

When an insect flies into a web, the spider darts out to bite its prey. As the spider bites, venom pumps out through its hollow fangs and enters the victim's body.

The venom stops the creature from moving and begins to digest its body, turning it into a kind of soup. Then the spider sucks up the liquid.

A spider will often wrap up its prey before it can get away.

Other spiders have fangs like daggers.

Some spiders have fangs like pincers.

Hunting prey

Not all spiders spin webs; some hunt for a meal. Jumping spiders are deadly hunters. They have amazing eyesight and can jump up to 50 times their body length to catch their prey.

A jumping spider prepares to pounce.

The fishing spider rests its legs on the surface of the water, feeling for the movement of tadpoles, frogs, and fish in the water below.

A fishing spider feels for prey in the water.

FACT ...

Net-casting spiders hold a small web between their legs and throw it over insects like a net.

Ambush!

Some spiders are sneaky hunters and ambush their prey. They hide somewhere safe and stay very still. Then, when they see their prey, they jump out and grab it!

A trapdoor spider grabs an unlucky insect.

The purse web spider hides in a long silk tube on the ground.

This crane fly has just been stabbed by a purse web spider from beneath.

The crab spider can change its color to match the petals on a flower. It hides inside flowers to catch insects that come to feed.

Can you spot the crab spider?

Deadly venom

Most spiders bite and have venom, but only about 100 species are dangerous to humans.

Spotlight: Black widow spider

Record breaker:	most venomous spider in U.S.
Leg span:	up to 1.5 in. (4cm)
Effect of venom:	causes breathing problems
Eats:	flies, mosquitoes, beetles

Spotlight: Brazilian wandering spider

Record breaker:	one of the most venomous
Leg span:	5 in. (12cm)
Effect of venom:	severe pain; death
Eats:	insects, other spiders, frogs

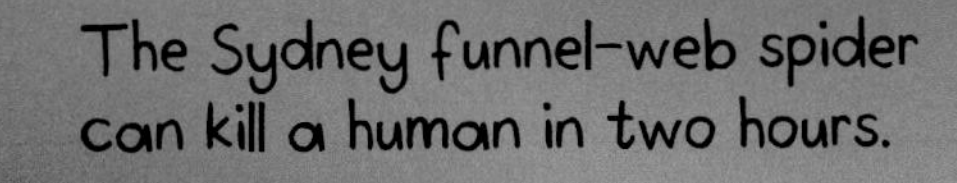
The Sydney funnel-web spider can kill a human in two hours.

Finding a mate

Most spiders live alone. When it is time to mate, a male finds a female by following the scent she leaves on her silk.

When the female lays her eggs, she wraps them in a thick cocoon and then puts them somewhere safe to hatch.

Mediterranean black widow spider

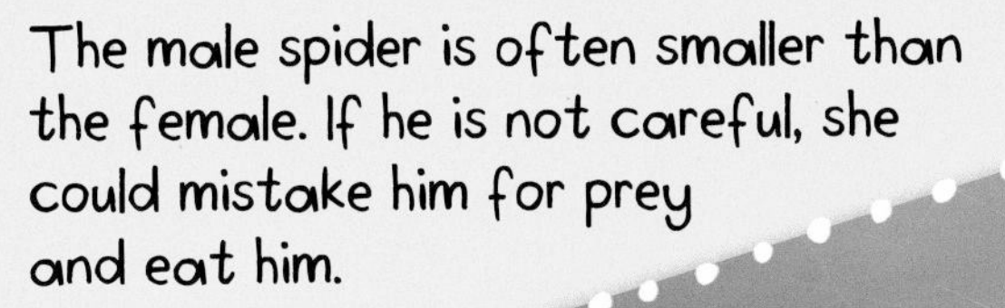

The male spider is often smaller than the female. If he is not careful, she could mistake him for prey and eat him.

golden orb weaver spiders

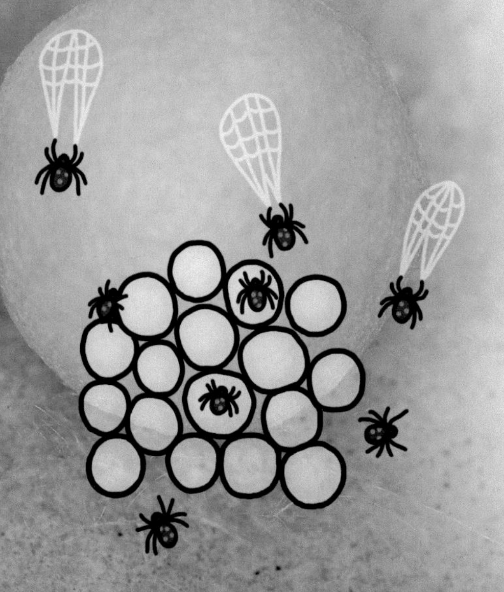

FACT ...

After mating once, the female black widow spider can lay eggs for the rest of her life.

Tiny wasp spiderlings hatch out together.

Spiderlings

Baby spiders are called spiderlings. They hatch out of their eggs together but soon spread out to look for food. If they didn't, they would eat one another!

Each tiny spiderling makes a line of very fine silk, called gossamer, and uses it to float away on the breeze. This is called ballooning.

Some spiderlings become caught up on airplanes; others float across the ocean to remote islands.

Unusually the wolf spider carries her spiderlings on her back.

Don't eat me!

Most spiders escape from their enemies by dropping away on a line of silk, but many spiders have found clever ways to hide. Some hold their front legs up like antennae and pretend to be ants or wasps. Others look like something nasty to eat.

An ant mimic spider pretends to be an ant.

The bird-dropping spider looks like . . .
a bird dropping!

FACT ...

The ladybug mimic spider is red with black spots and looks like a ladybug. The tree stump orb weaver spider looks like tree bark.

Lovely spiders

Many people do not like spiders, but they can help us. They eat pests in gardens and on farms. Scientists think spiders can help in other ways, too.

Roasted tarantulas have a nutty flavor.

Spiders eat pests such as grasshoppers.

Scientists study spider venom to see if they can use it to make insecticides that are less harmful to the planet.

Scientists in Germany work to copy spider silk.

FACT ...

Stories from thousands of years ago tell how people once used spiders' webs to help heal wounds.

GLOSSARY

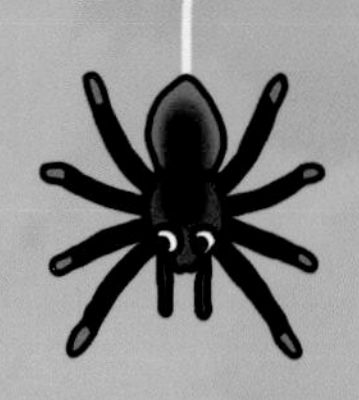

abdomen The back part of the body of spiders and other arachnids.

ambush To lie in wait and attack an animal by surprise.

Antarctica The ice-covered land around the South Pole.

antennae The pair of feelers on an insect's head.

arachnids A group of animals that have four pairs of legs and a body divided into two parts.

burrow A hole or tunnel dug by an animal for shelter.

cocoon The silky covering a spider spins to protect its eggs.

digest To break down food so that it can be used by the body.

insecticides The sprays and powders that farmers use to kill insect pests.

leg span The distance between two legs on the opposite sides of a spider.

orb web A web with a round, circular shape.

prey An animal that is hunted and killed by other animals for food.

segmented Made up of different parts or sections (segments).

species A group of living things that share similar features and can breed together.

spiderling A baby spider.

spinnerets The parts of a spider's body that produce silk.

venom The poison that a spider injects when it bites.

INDEX

abdomen 8
arachnids 6

babies 24–25
ballooning 24
bites 14, 20
black widow spiders 20, 22, 23

camouflage 26
cocoons 22

eggs 10, 22, 23, 24
exoskeleton 9
eyes 9

fangs 8, 14
food 5, 24
funnel-web spiders 21

garden spiders 11, 14

habitats 4
hairs 8
hunting 16–17

jumping spiders 10, 16, 17

legs 6, 7, 8, 9, 11, 17, 26

mating 22–23

orb weaver spiders 13, 23 27

pest control 28
prey 10, 14, 15, 16, 17, 18, 23

silk 7, 8, 10–11, 12, 14, 15, 19, 22, 24, 26, 29
species 4, 20
spiderlings 24–25
spinnerets 8, 11

tarantulas 5, 28
trapdoor spiders 18

venom 5, 8, 9, 14, 20–21, 29

webs 10, 12–13, 16, 17, 29

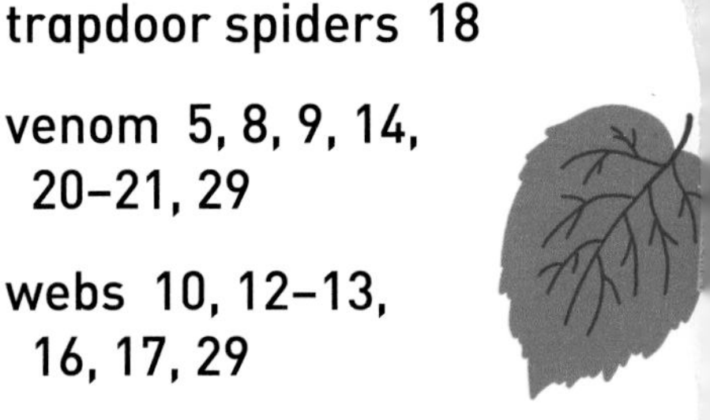